Harvesting your Truths

🌿 **Purple Affirmations**

Guided Affirmation & Reflection Book
A Soulful Journey to Plant Courage, Grow Purpose, and Bloom Legacy

---

by Dr. Rashonda Harris
Founder, Purple Sheep Consulting
Aim to Inspire, NOT compete!

♡ A Welcome Reflection by Dr. Rashonda Harris

"Every dream, every breakthrough, every act of courage begins the same way — with a single seed of belief. By opening these pages, you've made a powerful choice: to honor your growth, to trust your timing, and to harvest your truth.

This journey isn't about rushing to bloom — it's about planting with intention, nurturing with love, and rising with grace.

Let's sow boldly, water faithfully, and watch your harvest unfold."
— Dr. Rashonda Harris

Inside these pages, you'll:

✦ Receive 44 soulful affirmations rooted in growth, resilience, and divine purpose

🌱 Reflect on your personal journey through thought-provoking prompts

🪴 Strengthen your connection to your vision, voice, and legacy

🌀 Plant seeds of courage, self-trust, and transformative action

---

This is your soil.

Your season.

Your sacred harvest.

Welcome to your Truth. 🩶

🌿 Introduction: How to Use This Book

Before you begin this journey, it's important to align your heart with the energy woven through the *Purple Harvest* movement. This book is designed as a companion to your growth — not as a race, but as a rhythmic, soul-led walk through your personal field of becoming.

To fully connect with the spirit of these affirmations, it is recommended that you:
- ☑ Embrace each affirmation as a seed of power, courage, and purpose
- ☑ Take your time — one page, one reflection, one truth at a time
- ☑ Let your intuition guide your pace — daily, weekly, or as needed
- ☑ Pair this journey with the foundational principles found in *Purple Harvest: Planting Goals, Growing Truths*

Whether you are a Power Planter, Precision Planner, Dream Weaver, Root Builder — or your own evolving mix — this journey will help you:
- ☑ Anchor yourself more deeply in your truth
- ☑ Nurture resilience, clarity, and joy as daily practices
- ☑ Honor your personal growth as sacred work
- ☑ Trust that your harvest is already unfolding, one seed at a time

🌱 How It Works: • Each page contains one powerful affirmation + one gentle reflection prompt
• Allow the words to settle — read, breathe, reflect, and respond from your soul
• There is no rush — growth honors its own perfect timing
• Your reflections will become the living roots of your next season of blooming

This is more than an affirmation book — it's a place where your legacy begins to take deeper root.

🌱 Are you ready to harvest your truths?
Let's begin. 🖤

🌿 🩶 Affirmation 1

You are planting seeds today that generations will harvest tomorrow.

———

🌱 Reflection Prompt

What seeds am I planting right now that could impact others beyond me?

 Affirmation 2

Your truth is fertile ground. Trust what you are growing, even when it's still unseen.

— — —

Reflection Prompt

Where am I being called to trust my process even without immediate results?

 💜 Affirmation 3

Every step forward roots you deeper into purpose. Even slow growth is still growth.

— — —

🌱 Reflection Prompt

Where have I seen evidence that small steps led to big changes?

🌿 🖤 Affirmation 4

You are not behind. You are blooming exactly on time.

— — —

🌱 Reflection Prompt

What season am I currently in — planting, growing, blooming, or harvesting?

🌿 🩶 Affirmation 5

Purple Sheep don't chase seasons. They trust their harvest will come in divine timing.

— — —

🌱 Reflection Prompt

What have I been rushing that I need to surrender to divine timing?

 **Affirmation 6**

Your courage is the rain. Your vision is the sunlight. Your resilience is the soil.

🌱 Reflection Prompt

Which of these do I need to pour more into my dreams right now —
courage, vision, or resilience?

 **Affirmation 7**

The roots you plant in faith will bloom louder than any doubt spoken over you.

🌱 Reflection Prompt

Where have I overcome doubt before? What root of faith do I need to plant deeper today?

 **Affirmation 8**

Don't rush the soil. Some of the most powerful transformations happen underground first.

— — —

🌱 Reflection Prompt

What hidden growth am I currently experiencing?

 **Affirmation 9**

You were born to disrupt barren fields and plant new gardens of greatness.

— — —

🌱 Reflection Prompt

Where am I being called to plant something new — even if no one else sees it yet?

 🩶 Affirmation 10

Every "no" you survived was clearing the ground for your true harvest to take root.

— — —

🌱 Reflection Prompt

How have my setbacks prepared me for my harvest?

🌿 💜 Affirmation 11

You are the living proof that storms don't stop seeds — they strengthen them.

— — —

🌱 Reflection Prompt

What storm have I weathered that made me stronger than before?

 **Affirmation 12**

Patience is the silent partner of every great harvest.

🌱 Reflection Prompt

Where in my life am I being called to trust the process instead of rushing the result?

🌿 🖤 Affirmation 13

Your dreams are roots, stretching far beneath the surface before they bloom.

— — —

Reflection Prompt

What unseen work am I doing today that is preparing me for tomorrow?

🌿 💜 Affirmation 14

Even when the field looks empty, faith says, "Something beautiful is growing."

— — —

🌱 Reflection Prompt

Where in my life do I need to trust the seeds I've planted?

🌿 🩶 Affirmation 15

Harvests don't come from wishing. They come from working with heart and hope.

— — —

🌱 Reflection Prompt

How can I show up more fully for the dreams I say I want?

🌿 🤍 Affirmation 16

You are not meant to grow like anyone else. Your bloom will be your own.

— — —

🏺 Reflection Prompt

How can I honor my unique timeline instead of comparing it to others?

🌿 🩶 **Affirmation 17**

When others see a wasteland, you see a future forest.

— — —

🌱 Reflection Prompt

Where am I being called to plant hope where others have given up?

 **Affirmation 18**

Roots run deepest in seasons of quiet, not applause.

🌱 Reflection Prompt

How can I nurture my growth even when no one is watching?

🌿 🩶 Affirmation 19

Every "almost gave up" moment is a future harvest waiting to happen.

— — —

Reflection Prompt

What breakthrough might be waiting just beyond where I feel tired?

🌿 🩶 **Affirmation 20**

Some seasons are for planting. Some are for pruning. Both are preparing you.

— — —

🌱 Reflection Prompt

Am I being called to plant, to prune, or to harvest right now?

🌿 🖤 Affirmation 21

A Purple Sheep doesn't ask permission to bloom — they bloom because they were born to.

— — —

🌱 Reflection Prompt

Where in my life do I need to bloom boldly without waiting for approval?

🌿 💜 Affirmation 22

Legacy isn't built in a day — it's sown in daily, ordinary acts of courage.

— — —

🌱 Reflection Prompt

What small, courageous seed can I plant today toward the legacy I want to leave?

🌿 🩶 Affirmation 23

Your quiet seasons are not empty; they are sacred spaces where strength is built.

— — —

Reflection Prompt

How can I honor the unseen seasons of my journey with more grace?

🌱 🩶 Affirmation 24

The seeds you plant in faith will outgrow the weeds planted in fear.

🌱 Reflection Prompt

What seeds of faith am I being called to water right now?

🌿 🩶 Affirmation 25

You are allowed to outgrow spaces that once felt like home.

— — —

Reflection Prompt

What spaces or mindsets have I outgrown, and what am I growing toward?

🌿 🤍 Affirmation 26

Sometimes the greatest gift you can give yourself is permission to begin again.

— — —

🌱 Reflection Prompt

Where am I being invited to offer myself a fresh start?

🌿 🖤 Affirmation 27

Not every seed you plant will bloom — but every bloom begins with a planted seed.

— — —

🌱 Reflection Prompt

How can I release the need for guarantees and trust the planting anyway?

🌱 🤍 **Affirmation 28**

In every ending, there is soil rich enough for new beginnings.

— — —

🌱 Reflection Prompt

What new beginning is quietly asking for my attention right now?

🌿 🖤 Affirmation 29

The deeper your roots, the wider your reach will become.

— — —

Reflection Prompt

What roots am I nurturing to support the life I'm building?

🌿 🩶 Affirmation 30

Your future harvest depends more on your faithfulness than your feelings.

— — —

🌱 Reflection Prompt

How can I stay faithful to my vision even when motivation fades?

🌿 💚 Affirmation 31

Trust the journey — every detour still leads to destiny.

— — —

🌱 Reflection Prompt

Where have unexpected turns led me closer to my purpose?

 **Affirmation 32**

The universe doesn't recognize hurry — only heart.

— — —

🌱 Reflection Prompt

How can I shift from rushing to rooting myself deeper in my purpose?

🌱 🩶 Affirmation 33

The seeds you plant in self-love will bloom in every area of your life.

— — —

🌱 Reflection Prompt

What act of self-love can I plant today for tomorrow's growth?

🌿 🩶 Affirmation 34

You were born to be fruitful — not frantic.

— — —

🌱 Reflection Prompt

Where can I choose fruitful focus over frantic striving today?

🌿 🩶 Affirmation 35

You are not behind; you are being prepared for what you were built to carry.

— — —

🌱 Reflection Prompt

How can I honor the preparation season I'm in, even when it feels slow?

🌿 🩶 Affirmation 36

Your gifts are seeds the world desperately needs — plant them boldly.

— — —

🌱 Reflection Prompt

What gift have I been hesitant to plant, and how can I share it with boldness?

🌿 🖤 Affirmation 37

Every season of struggle is loosening the soil for your next season of bloom.

— — —

🌱 Reflection Prompt

What struggles are preparing me for a stronger harvest ahead?

🌿 💜 Affirmation 38

A Purple Sheep doesn't just survive the seasons — they thrive through them.

— — —

🌱 Reflection Prompt

Where in my life am I being called to not just survive, but to thrive?

🌿 🩶 Affirmation 39

Joy is fertilizer for your dreams. Protect it fiercely.

— — —

🌱 Reflection Prompt

How can I intentionally protect and nurture my joy this week?

🌿 💜 Affirmation 40

Purpose doesn't panic under pressure. It deepens its roots.

— — —

🌱 Reflection Prompt

How can I stay rooted when challenges try to shake me?

🌿 🩶 Affirmation 41

Your energy is a garden — plant what you want to grow.

— — —

🌱 Reflection Prompt

What thoughts, habits, or relationships am I nurturing with my energy?

🌿 🖤 Affirmation 42

A seed only needs one thing to break ground: belief.

— — —

🌱 Reflection Prompt

Where am I being asked to believe deeper than I can currently see?

🌿 💜 Affirmation 43

You are both the gardener and the garden — tend to yourself with patience and pride.

— — —

Reflection Prompt

How can I tend to my own growth with more love and consistency?

🌿 🩶 Affirmation 44

Your harvest will be proof that nothing planted with love is ever wasted.

— — —

🌱 Reflection Prompt

What seed of love have I planted that I am trusting will bloom in divine time?

🌿 You didn't just read affirmations — you planted seeds of courage, trust, and resilience.

Each reflection was a watering moment.
Each page was a choice to believe a little deeper in yourself.
Each quiet answer you gave was a root taking hold in sacred ground.

You are not who you were when you began this journey.
You have harvested new rhythms of thought, new waves of purpose, and new branches of becoming.

The seeds you've planted will continue to bloom in ways you can't yet imagine.

Nurture them.
Trust them.
Let them surprise you.

You are living proof that truth, when planted with love, never returns void.
A new beginning didn't wait for permission — you just gave it to yourself.

— Dr. Rashonda Harris

"Keep planting. Keep rising. Your harvest is already unfolding."

Made in the USA
Middletown, DE
07 June 2025

76687637R00053